Dean & Torvill's Final Dance

The most famous figure skating couple, who announced their retirement on the 40th anniversary of their Olympic gold medal, takes us on a journey through their grace, grit, and grandeur.

Beatrice Holland

Table of Contents

Introduction

Ice skating enthusiasts and sports aficionados alike have witnessed the magic created by the legendary duo, Jayne Torvill and Christopher Dean. Their names are synonymous with grace, precision, and a transformative impact on the world of ice dancing. As we delve into their remarkable journey, it's essential to understand the background that shaped Torvill and Dean's rise to fame, the profound significance of the 40th anniversary of their Olympic gold, and the overarching purpose of this book.

Background of Torvill and Dean

Jayne Torvill and Christopher Dean, hailing from Nottingham, England, embarked on their skating journey at an early age. Born on

October 7, 1957, Jayne Torvill displayed an innate talent for figure skating, while Christopher Dean, born on July 27, 1958, showcased his prowess on the ice from a young age. Their paths converged when they teamed up as a skating pair in 1975, marking the beginning of a partnership that would etch their names in the annals of ice dancing history.

Torvill and Dean's synchronized movements, intricate choreography, and a seamless blend of athleticism and artistry set them apart from their contemporaries. As they honed their skills and ascended the ranks, it became evident that this duo was destined for greatness. Their commitment to pushing the boundaries of ice dancing, exploring new forms of expression, and captivating audiences with their performances laid the foundation for an extraordinary career.

Significance of the 40th Anniversary

The 40th anniversary of Torvill and Dean's Olympic gold medal in Sarajevo holds profound significance in the narrative of their illustrious careers. It marks four decades since that unforgettable moment on February 14, 1984, when they dazzled the world with their flawless interpretation of Maurice Ravel's Bolero. This iconic performance not only secured them a gold medal but also left an indelible mark on the sport of ice dancing.

The anniversary serves as a poignant milestone, inviting reflection on the impact of their legacy, the evolution of ice dancing since that historic day, and the enduring inspiration they've provided to generations of skaters. It's a moment to celebrate not just a victory in a competition but a triumph that transcends time, resonating with fans and skaters around the world who continue to be captivated by the magic of Torvill and Dean's Bolero routine.

Purpose of the Book

As we embark on this exploration of Torvill and Dean's journey, it's crucial to clarify the purpose that drives the pages of this book. Beyond a mere recounting of their achievements, the purpose is to delve into the multifaceted aspects of their careers, the impact they've had on the sport of ice dancing, and the broader cultural significance of their contributions.

This book aims to provide a comprehensive and insightful narrative that goes beyond the surface, offering readers a deeper understanding of the duo's artistry, dedication, and the challenges they overcame. It seeks to capture the essence of Torvill and Dean's influence not only within the realm of competitive skating but also in popularizing the sport and breaking new ground in artistic expression.

Furthermore, the book strives to showcase the enduring relevance of Torvill and Dean's legacy. By examining their journey from the early years in Nottingham to the pinnacle of Olympic success and their subsequent ventures, readers will gain a holistic perspective on the profound impact this duo has had on the world of ice skating.

In essence, the purpose of this book is to pay homage to two individuals whose passion for their craft transcended the boundaries of competition and left an indelible mark on the hearts of those who witnessed their performances. Through meticulous research, personal insights, and reflections from those influenced by their work, we aim to create a narrative that captures the essence of Torvill and Dean's extraordinary contribution to the world of ice dancing. As we turn the pages, we invite readers to join us on a journey through time, reliving the moments that defined an era in ice skating and celebrating the unparalleled artistry of Jayne Torvill and Christopher Dean.

Chapter 1: The Olympic Triumph

The pinnacle of Jayne Torvill and Christopher Dean's illustrious career came in the frosty confines of Sarajevo during the 1984 Winter Olympics. Their flawless execution of Maurice Ravel's Bolero not only secured them a gold medal but also etched their names in the annals of Olympic history. This section delves into the magic of their Bolero routine, its profound impact on British sporting history, and the enduring legacy that continues to inspire generations of skaters.

Sarajevo 1984: The Bolero Routine

On February 14, 1984, Torvill and Dean took to the ice in Sarajevo, Yugoslavia, for the free dance segment of the ice dancing competition. The atmosphere was charged with anticipation as the Nottingham duo began their mesmerizing performance to the haunting notes of Ravel's Bolero. What unfolded on that icy stage was nothing short of a masterpiece.

The Bolero routine, choreographed by Christopher Dean himself, was a triumph of artistic expression and technical precision. Each glide, each turn, and each lift were executed with an unparalleled grace that left the audience spellbound. The chemistry between Torvill and Dean was palpable, transcending the boundaries of a mere athletic performance to become a captivating dance narrative.

The routine, set against the backdrop of the dramatic Bolero music, built with intensity as the skaters moved seamlessly across the ice.

The lifts, spins, and intricate footwork were perfectly synchronized, creating a visual spectacle that resonated with both the judges and the spectators. As the final notes echoed through the arena, the audience erupted in applause, and the judges responded with a rare unanimous decision – perfect scores of 6.0 from all 12 judges.

Sarajevo 1984 was not just a competition; it was a moment frozen in time, encapsulating the zenith of Torvill and Dean's artistic prowess. The Bolero routine transcended the confines of figure skating, becoming a cultural phenomenon that captured the imagination of people worldwide.

Impact on British Sporting History

The significance of Torvill and Dean's Olympic triumph extends far beyond the confines of the ice rink. The gold medal in Sarajevo marked a watershed moment in British sporting history, elevating ice dancing to a level of prominence previously unseen in the country.

Prior to their triumph, ice dancing had often been overshadowed by other winter sports in the UK. Torvill and Dean's success not only brought the sport into the national spotlight but also ignited a renewed interest in figure skating. Their victory inspired a generation of young skaters across Britain, laying the groundwork for a flourishing ice dancing community.

The impact on British sporting history went beyond the immediate aftermath of the 1984 Olympics. Torvill and Dean became trailblazers, breaking down barriers and proving that excellence in winter sports was not exclusive to nations with a long history of icy traditions. Their success paved the way for increased support and recognition of winter sports in the UK, fostering a new era of athletes aspiring to follow in their footsteps.

Legacy and Inspiration

The legacy of Torvill and Dean's Bolero routine endures as a testament to the transformative power of artistry in sport. Beyond the medals and accolades, they left an indelible mark on the world of ice dancing, influencing the evolution of the discipline. Their ability to seamlessly blend technical proficiency with artistic expression set a standard that many aspire to achieve.

The Bolero routine continues to be studied and revered by aspiring skaters and coaches worldwide. Its timeless elegance and emotional depth serve as a source of inspiration, encouraging skaters to push the boundaries of creativity and storytelling within the confines of competitive routines. Torvill and Dean's legacy in this regard goes beyond their own achievements, as they have become influential figures in the broader context of figure skating history.

The inspiration derived from Torvill and Dean's Bolero routine extends beyond the ice rink. Their success narrative, marked by dedication, resilience, and a pursuit of artistic excellence, has motivated individuals in various fields. The enduring image of their Olympic triumph serves as a reminder that greatness is achievable through a combination of skill, passion, and unwavering commitment to one's craft.

In conclusion, Torvill and Dean's Olympic triumph in Sarajevo was a defining moment not only for their careers but also for the landscape of ice dancing and British sports as a whole. The Bolero routine remains a symbol of artistic perfection, and its impact resonates through the years, inspiring a legacy that transcends the boundaries of competitive figure skating. As we celebrate the 40th anniversary of this historic event, we continue to marvel at the artistry, grace, and enduring inspiration that Torvill and Dean brought to the world of sports.

Chapter 2:Professional Journey

Transition to Professional Skating

Following their triumph at the 1984 Winter Olympics, Torvill and Dean made the pivotal decision to transition from the competitive circuit to the world of professional skating. This move allowed them the freedom to explore new artistic dimensions, unburdened by the constraints of mandatory figures and prescribed routines. It was a shift that not only showcased their versatility but also opened doors to a broader audience.

Embracing their newfound status as professionals, Torvill and Dean embarked on a journey that would see them tour the world, captivating audiences with their mesmerizing performances. The transition allowed them to experiment with different styles, music genres, and choreographic elements that went beyond the parameters of competitive routines. Their ability to connect with audiences on a more personal level became a hallmark of their professional endeavors.

The professional phase of their career was marked by collaborations with renowned choreographers and musicians, expanding the horizons of ice dancing as an art form. Torvill and Dean's performances during this period were not just about executing technical elements; they became immersive experiences that blended athleticism with storytelling, showcasing the emotive power of figure skating.

Winning Bronze at the 1994 Winter Olympics

While their transition to professional skating was a testament to their artistic evolution, Torvill and Dean surprised the world by returning to competitive ice for the 1994 Winter Olympics in Lillehammer, Norway. This decision marked a unique chapter in their careers, and their performance garnered attention for its poignancy and grace.

Competing against a new generation of skaters, Torvill and Dean presented a routine that combined their signature artistry with a maturity and depth that came from years of experience. The result was a bronze medal, a remarkable achievement considering the changing landscape of competitive figure skating.

The significance of winning bronze in Lillehammer lay not just in the medal itself but in the narrative it added to Torvill and Dean's legacy. It showcased their enduring commitment to the sport, their ability to adapt to changing times, and the timeless quality of their performances. The bronze medal was not merely an addition to their collection; it was a testament to their resilience and the lasting impact they continued to have on the world of figure skating.

Evolution of Torvill and Dean's Skating Style

The evolution of Torvill and Dean's skating style throughout their professional journey is a captivating exploration of artistic growth and innovation. Moving beyond the structured routines of competitive skating, they embraced a more nuanced and expressive approach, pushing the boundaries of what was considered traditional in figure skating.

In their professional career, Torvill and Dean's skating style became a canvas for experimentation. They seamlessly blended classical and contemporary elements, incorporating diverse music genres into their routines. This fusion of styles not only showcased their technical prowess but also highlighted their ability to connect with audiences emotionally. Each performance became a storytelling experience, with the ice serving as a stage for narratives that ranged from the classical to the avant-garde.

The evolution of their skating style was also evident in their collaborations with prominent choreographers. Working with creative minds in the industry allowed Torvill and Dean to explore new dimensions of movement, challenging conventional notions of what figure skating could achieve. This innovative spirit not only kept their performances fresh and engaging but also contributed to the broader evolution of ice dancing as an art form.

As they continued to tour and perform, Torvill and Dean's skating style became a synthesis of their collective experiences. The technical precision honed during their competitive years melded seamlessly with the expressive freedom of their professional phase, creating a unique blend that resonated with audiences worldwide.

In conclusion, the professional journey of Jayne Torvill and Christopher Dean is a testament to the transformative power of artistic exploration in figure skating. Their transition to professional skating allowed them to break free from the constraints of competition, opening doors to new possibilities and paving the way for a redefined skating style. From winning bronze at the 1994 Winter Olympics to the continuous evolution of their skating style, Torvill and Dean's professional journey is a rich tapestry of creativity, resilience, and a commitment to pushing the boundaries of their craft.

Chapter 3: Dancing On Ice

ITV's Dancing On Ice: Torvill and Dean as Icons

In 2006, the landscape of British television was transformed with the debut of ITV's Dancing On Ice, a reality show that brought the elegance and excitement of figure skating to a mainstream audience. At the heart of this televised spectacle were the two figures synonymous with ice dancing excellence – Jayne Torvill and Christopher Dean. Their presence as professional coaches and mentors elevated the show to new heights and added a touch of authenticity that resonated with viewers.

As icons of the sport, Torvill and Dean brought a wealth of experience and expertise to Dancing On Ice. Their role as mentors extended beyond coaching technical elements; it was about imparting the essence of performance, storytelling, and the emotional connection that makes figure skating a captivating art form. Contestants on the show not only received guidance in perfecting their jumps and spins but also benefited from the wisdom of two individuals whose names are etched in the history of figure skating.

The chemistry between Torvill and Dean on the show mirrored the magic they created on the ice during their competitive years. Their camaraderie, shared laughter, and genuine passion for the sport endeared them to audiences. The presence of these two icons not only lent credibility to the show but also made it a celebration of figure skating as an accessible and thrilling form of entertainment.

Head Judges and Beyond

As Dancing On Ice gained popularity, Torvill and Dean's roles evolved, propelling them from mentors to head judges. Their transition to the judging panel was a natural progression, as their discerning eyes and extensive knowledge of the sport made them invaluable critics. As head judges, Torvill and Dean brought a combination of technical precision and artistic appreciation to the show, offering constructive feedback that went beyond the realm of a typical reality competition.

In their roles as head judges, Torvill and Dean became the faces of authority and expertise in the world of Dancing On Ice. Their critiques were insightful, offering contestants not just a score but also valuable insights into how they could elevate their performances. This added a layer of authenticity to the judging process, as the contestants were evaluated by individuals who had not only mastered the technical aspects of skating but had also shaped the very landscape of ice dancing.

The transition to head judges also showcased Torvill and Dean's commitment to nurturing the next generation of skaters. Their mentorship extended beyond the training rink to the television screen, where they played a pivotal role in shaping the careers of aspiring figure skaters. The genuine interest they showed in the contestants' journeys, coupled with their constructive criticism, created an environment where the artistry and athleticism of figure skating were celebrated.

Impact on the Popularity of Ice Skating

Dancing On Ice emerged as a cultural phenomenon, captivating audiences across demographics and rekindling a fascination with figure skating. Torvill and Dean's presence on the show played a crucial role in this resurgence of interest in ice skating as a televised sport. Their ability to demystify the complexities of figure skating and make it accessible to a wider audience contributed significantly to the show's success.

The impact of Dancing On Ice on the popularity of ice skating extended beyond the confines of the television screen. It sparked a renewed interest in the sport at a grassroots level, inspiring individuals to take up figure skating and explore the joy of gliding on ice. Skating rinks saw an uptick in attendance, and figure skating clubs experienced a surge in membership as the show reignited a passion for the sport.

Furthermore, the show's format, which paired celebrities with professional figure skaters, highlighted the discipline and artistry required in figure skating. It humanized the sport, showcasing the challenges and triumphs of individuals who ventured into the world of figure skating without prior experience. Torvill and Dean's mentorship added credibility to this narrative, emphasizing the transformative power of dedication and hard work in mastering the intricacies of figure skating.

In conclusion, Dancing On Ice, with Jayne Torvill and Christopher Dean as icons and head judges, not only brought the elegance of figure skating to the forefront of British television but also played a pivotal role in rekindling public interest in the sport. Their mentorship and constructive criticism contributed to the show's authenticity, making it a celebration of the artistry and athleticism that defines figure skating. The impact of Dancing On Ice reverberated far beyond the confines of the television screen, inspiring a new generation of skaters and reaffirming the timeless allure of ice dancing as a captivating form of entertainment.

Chapter 4: The Decision to Retire

Reflecting on Their Career

As Torvill and Dean approach the twilight of their competitive careers, the decision to retire prompts a reflection on the extraordinary journey that has defined their lives. With a career that began in the mid-1970s, they have been pioneers in the world of ice dancing, leaving an indelible mark on the sport. Reflecting on their career involves revisiting the highs and lows, the triumphs and challenges that have shaped their narrative.

The mirror of retrospection reveals a tapestry of achievements that includes the iconic Bolero routine at the 1984 Winter Olympics, multiple world championship titles, and a bronze medal at the 1994 Winter Olympics. Beyond the medals and accolades, Torvill and Dean's career has been characterized by innovation, artistic brilliance, and a commitment to pushing the boundaries of their craft.

The decision to retire is not just about acknowledging the past but also recognizing the impact they have had on the sport and the countless lives they have inspired. It's a moment of introspection that encompasses not only their achievements on the ice but also their contributions to the broader cultural landscape, from professional skating to their roles as head judges on Dancing On Ice.

Timing and Decision-Making

Timing is a crucial element in the decision to retire, and for Torvill and Dean, the announcement comes as a thoughtful and considered choice. The timing is not just a matter of chronological markers but a recognition of the physical and emotional demands of competitive ice skating. As they gracefully enter their mid-sixties, the decision to retire is a culmination of factors, including the natural progression of age and a desire to conclude their competitive careers on their own terms.

The decision-making process likely involved a delicate balance between the love for their craft and a pragmatic acknowledgment of the realities of aging. Competitive ice skating demands a level of physical prowess and agility that may diminish with time, and the decision to retire is a testament to their respect for the integrity of the sport and their desire to step down while still maintaining a certain level of performance.

Beyond the physical considerations, the decision-making process also encompasses a range of emotional and personal factors. It involves evaluating the passion for the sport, the joy derived from performing, and the fulfillment that comes from a lifetime dedicated to figure skating. The timing, therefore, becomes a convergence of physical readiness, emotional well-being, and a keen understanding of their own legacy within the sport.

Nostalgia and New Beginnings

The decision to retire is inherently bittersweet, a delicate interplay between nostalgia for the past and the anticipation of new beginnings.

Nostalgia, in this context, is rooted in the memories of triumphs and challenges, the exhilaration of standing on the Olympic podium, and the enduring impact of performances that have left an indelible mark on the hearts of fans worldwide.

The Bolero routine, which garnered perfect scores at the 1984 Winter Olympics, stands as a poignant symbol of their legacy. Nostalgia encapsulates the echoes of that performance, the cheers of the crowd, and the profound sense of accomplishment that followed. The decision to retire is an acknowledgment of the nostalgia that surrounds these moments, a recognition that the time has come to conclude a chapter that has defined a significant portion of their lives.

Simultaneously, retirement is a gateway to new beginnings. It opens doors to fresh pursuits, whether they involve mentoring the next generation of skaters, exploring choreography, or simply enjoying a different pace of life. The decision to retire is not an endpoint but a threshold to embrace the possibilities that lie beyond the competitive ice skating arena.

New beginnings also extend to the fans and the broader figure skating community. The legacy of Torvill and Dean will continue to inspire future generations of skaters, coaches, and enthusiasts. The decision to retire is an invitation for the skating world to celebrate the past while eagerly anticipating what the future holds. It sets the stage for a new generation to take center ice and continue pushing the boundaries of artistic expression and athletic prowess.

In conclusion, the decision to retire for Jayne Torvill and Christopher Dean is a multifaceted process that involves introspection, thoughtful timing, and a delicate balance between nostalgia and new beginnings. As they gracefully exit the competitive ice skating arena, their legacy remains intact, and the echoes of their performances will resonate for years to come. The retirement announcement is not just an endpoint but a transition, a turning of the page to the next chapter in the remarkable story of two individuals who have left an indelible mark on the world of figure skating.

Chapter 5: Torvill & Dean: Our Last Dance Tour

Overview of the Farewell Tour

"Our Last Dance" is more than just a tour; it is a symbolic celebration of Torvill and Dean's enduring legacy in the world of figure skating. The tour, scheduled to run from April 12 to May 11, 2025, is a carefully crafted journey that encapsulates the essence of their careers. It is a farewell to the stage that has witnessed the magic of their performances and a tribute to the fans who have supported them through every twirl and lift.

The choice of the title, "Our Last Dance," reflects a poetic acknowledgment of the finality of this tour. It is an invitation for audiences to join Torvill and Dean in a dance that transcends the physical movements on the ice – a dance that encapsulates the emotions, memories, and the collective experience of a partnership that has left an indelible mark on figure skating history.

The tour is not just a sequence of performances but a narrative that unfolds in multiple acts, each representing a phase of their careers. From the elegance of their early routines to the innovation of their professional years, the tour is a comprehensive retrospective that spans the entirety of Torvill and Dean's journey. It is a visual and emotional journey through time, a living testament to the artistry and grace that has defined their partnership.

Highlights and Expectations

As anticipation builds for "Our Last Dance," the tour promises to be a spectacle that transcends the boundaries of a typical ice skating performance. The highlights are expected to be a culmination of their most iconic routines, revisited with a touch of nostalgia and presented with the seasoned artistry that comes from years of experience. The tour is an opportunity for Torvill and Dean to showcase the full breadth of their repertoire, from the perfect Bolero that earned them Olympic gold to the innovative routines that characterized their professional years.

Expectations are high not just for the technical brilliance that audiences have come to associate with Torvill and Dean but also for the emotional resonance that their performances evoke. Each glide and lift is anticipated to be infused with the depth of their shared history, creating an atmosphere that is as much about storytelling as it is about athleticism. The tour is expected to be a celebration of their versatility, from classical elegance to contemporary innovation, demonstrating the evolution of their skating style over the years.

Collaborations with fellow skaters and artists are also expected to be a highlight of the tour. Torvill and Dean, known for their ability to seamlessly blend with partners and collaborators, are likely to share the stage with individuals who have been part of their journey. This collaborative element adds an extra layer of richness to the performances, showcasing not only their individual artistry but also the collective magic that happens when skaters come together.

The tour is not just about looking back; it is also an opportunity for Torvill and Dean to present new, innovative routines. While the majority of the performances are expected to be nostalgic revisitations of their classic routines, the inclusion of fresh, upbeat dances adds an element of surprise and excitement. It is a testament to their enduring creativity and a commitment to leaving audiences with lasting memories from their final tour.

Farewell to the Fans

The farewell tour is not just a goodbye to the stage; it is a heartfelt farewell to the fans who have been an integral part of Torvill and Dean's journey. The audiences who have cheered, applauded, and celebrated their performances over the years are invited to join them in this final dance. The tour becomes a shared experience, a collective celebration of the bond between performers and their admirers.

The farewell to the fans is likely to be an emotional journey, with moments of reflection and gratitude interspersed throughout the performances. Torvill and Dean, known for their connection with the audience, are expected to share personal anecdotes, express their appreciation for the unwavering support, and perhaps even engage in moments of intimacy that transcend the traditional performer-audience dynamic.

The tour is an opportunity for fans to not only witness the technical brilliance of Torvill and Dean one last time but also to be part of a communal experience that transcends the confines of the ice rink. It is a farewell that extends beyond the physical presence of the performers, resonating in the hearts of fans who have been touched by the magic of Torvill and Dean's performances.

In conclusion, "Our Last Dance" is a culmination of Torvill and Dean's extraordinary careers, a farewell tour that encapsulates the essence of their journey in figure skating. As they take their final bows on the ice, the tour becomes a celebration of artistry, athleticism, and the enduring bond between performers and fans. It is a poignant farewell that marks the end of a chapter in the history of figure skating, leaving behind a legacy that will continue to inspire generations to come.

Chapter 6: The Bolero Legacy

Analyzing the Iconic Routine

The Bolero routine, performed by Torvill and Dean at the 1984 Winter Olympics in Sarajevo, stands as a masterpiece of figure skating choreography. Choreographed by Christopher Dean himself, the routine was set to Maurice Ravel's haunting composition "Bolero." What unfolded on the ice was not just a sequence of jumps, spins, and lifts but a narrative woven through movement, emotion, and music.

The routine began with Torvill and Dean standing motionless on the ice, creating an immediate sense of anticipation. As the first notes of Bolero echoed through the arena, they initiated a slow, deliberate glide, building an atmosphere of suspense. The simplicity of their movements in the initial moments heightened the impact of what was to follow.

The choreography unfolded with precision and grace, each movement seamlessly connected to the music. The lifts were executed with effortless fluidity, spins were perfectly synchronized, and every gesture carried emotional weight. The routine built in intensity, mirroring the crescendo of the Bolero music. As they approached the final moments, Torvill and Dean maintained a captivating connection, embodying the passion and drama of the music.

The beauty of the Bolero routine lay not only in its technical perfection but in the storytelling aspect. Torvill and Dean transformed the ice into a stage where the narrative of love and longing unfolded. The simplicity of the story, combined with the power of their execution, created a performance that resonated with audiences on a profound level.

Perfect Scores and Lasting Impact

The Bolero routine's impact was underscored by the unprecedented perfect scores it received from all twelve judges at the 1984 Winter Olympics. Achieving perfection in figure skating is a rare feat, and Torvill and Dean's Bolero remains the only performance in Olympic history to receive unanimous perfect scores.

The perfect scores were not just a testament to the technical excellence displayed by Torvill and Dean; they were a recognition of the transformative power of their artistry. The Bolero routine went beyond the confines of a competitive performance; it became a cultural touchstone that captured the imagination of people around the world. The perfect scores elevated Torvill and Dean to legendary status, solidifying their place in the pantheon of figure skating greats.

The impact of the perfect scores resonated far beyond the Olympic arena. It ignited a renewed interest in figure skating, drawing attention to the sport on a global scale. The Bolero routine became a symbol of excellence, inspiring a new generation of skaters to pursue the artistry and precision that characterized Torvill and Dean's performance.

Decades after their historic achievement, the Bolero routine continues to be a reference point in discussions about figure skating. It is a performance that has stood the test of time, remaining relevant and influential in a sport that constantly evolves. The perfect scores bestowed upon Torvill and Dean's Bolero remain a benchmark against which other figure skating performances are measured.

Contributions to Ice Dance Choreography

The Bolero routine's legacy extends beyond its perfect scores and cultural impact; it has left an indelible mark on the choreography of ice dance. Torvill and Dean's innovative approach to choreography in the Bolero routine challenged conventions and set new standards for what could be achieved on the ice.

The routine demonstrated a fusion of classical and contemporary elements, seamlessly blending traditional figure skating moves with expressive and emotionally charged gestures.

This blend of styles became a hallmark of Torvill and Dean's choreography, influencing subsequent generations of ice dancers to experiment with a diverse range of movements and music genres.

The Bolero routine's impact on ice dance choreography is evident in the increased emphasis on storytelling and emotion in performances. Torvill and Dean proved that figure skating could be more than a display of technical prowess; it could be a form of artistic expression that resonates with audiences on a visceral level. Ice dancers began to explore narratives within their routines, creating performances that engaged both the intellect and the emotions.

Furthermore, the Bolero routine inspired skaters to push the boundaries of what was considered possible in ice dance. The lifts and spins in the routine showcased a level of creativity and innovation that challenged preconceived notions of what could be achieved on the ice. Torvill and Dean's willingness to take risks in their choreography encouraged subsequent generations to explore new forms of movement and expression.

In conclusion, the Bolero routine's legacy is multifaceted, encompassing its status as an iconic performance, the perfect scores it garnered, and its lasting impact on ice dance choreography. Decades after its debut, Torvill and Dean's Bolero remains a symbol of artistic excellence and a source of inspiration for skaters and fans alike. It is a testament to the transformative power of figure skating when elevated to the level of art, a legacy that continues to influence and shape the landscape of the sport.

Chapter 7: Beyond the Ice Rink

Torvill and Dean's Influence Beyond Skating

Torvill and Dean's influence transcends the confines of the ice rink, reaching into diverse realms of society. Their partnership, marked by a seamless blend of athleticism and artistry, has served as a source of inspiration for individuals from various walks of life. Their impact extends beyond the realm of figure skating, resonating with those who admire not just their technical prowess but also their ability to tell compelling stories through movement.

One of the ways Torvill and Dean have influenced individuals beyond skating is through their roles as mentors and judges on

ITV's Dancing On Ice. As the faces of the show, they became household names and played a pivotal role in bringing figure skating to a broader audience. Their mentorship went beyond the technical aspects of skating; it became a source of guidance and encouragement for contestants navigating the challenges of competition.

Furthermore, Torvill and Dean's journey from competitors to professionals to head judges reflects a versatility that has inspired individuals to embrace change and evolution in their own lives. Their ability to seamlessly transition between roles within the skating world serves as a model for adaptability and continuous growth.

In the realm of sports, Torvill and Dean's impact is not limited to figure skating enthusiasts. Their dedication, discipline, and pursuit of excellence stand as universal principles applicable to any athletic endeavor. They have become role models for aspiring athletes, illustrating that success is not solely measured by medals but also by the enduring passion and commitment one brings to their craft.

Contributions to the Arts and Culture

Torvill and Dean's contributions to the arts and culture extend beyond their performances on the ice. As ambassadors for figure skating, they have played a crucial role in elevating the status of the sport to an art form. Their ability to infuse storytelling, emotion, and creativity into their routines has broadened the perception of figure skating as more than a competitive endeavor.

Their influence in the arts is also evident in their collaborations with choreographers and musicians. Working with creative minds, Torvill and Dean have pushed the boundaries of traditional figure skating routines, incorporating diverse music genres and innovative choreography. This willingness to experiment and explore new avenues has had a ripple effect, encouraging skaters and choreographers to embrace a broader spectrum of artistic expression.

Torvill and Dean's impact on culture extends to their contributions to popularizing figure skating as entertainment. Their involvement in ITV's Dancing On Ice brought figure skating into the living rooms of millions, fostering a renewed appreciation for the sport. The show's success attests to their ability to make figure skating accessible to a wider audience, contributing to the cultural landscape and creating a platform for the convergence of sport and entertainment.

Beyond the ice rink, Torvill and Dean's cultural impact is evident in the incorporation of figure skating into various forms of media and popular culture. References to their iconic Bolero routine can be found in films, television shows, and even commercials, showcasing the enduring influence of their performances on the collective imagination.

Enduring Impact on Future Generations

Perhaps the most enduring aspect of Torvill and Dean's legacy is the impact they have had on future generations of figure skaters and athletes. As trailblazers in the world of ice dancing, they have inspired countless individuals to pursue their passion for figure skating and to approach their craft with dedication and creativity.

Their influence on future generations is palpable in the evolving landscape of figure skating. Skaters who grew up watching Torvill and Dean have incorporated elements of their style into their own performances, creating a stylistic continuum that connects past and present. The Bolero routine, in particular, continues to serve as a touchstone for skaters aspiring to achieve the perfect blend of technical precision and emotional storytelling.

Torvill and Dean's impact on young skaters is not only technical but also philosophical. They have instilled a belief in the transformative power of dedication and hard work, emphasizing that success in any field requires not only talent but also resilience and perseverance. Their journey, from the humble beginnings in Nottingham to the pinnacle of Olympic glory, serves as a narrative of inspiration for those dreaming of achieving greatness in their own pursuits.

The establishment of the Torvill and Dean International Skating Academy further cements their commitment to nurturing the next generation of skaters. Through coaching and mentorship, they continue to impart their knowledge and experience, shaping the future of figure skating. The academy serves as a testament to their dedication to passing on the torch and ensuring that the sport evolves with the same spirit of innovation and excellence they brought to it.

In conclusion, Jayne Torvill and Christopher Dean's influence extends far beyond the realm of figure skating. Their impact on arts, culture, and future generations is a testament to the enduring power of their partnership. As they gracefully exit the competitive stage, their legacy remains a guiding light for those who seek to excel not just in the world of sports but in any endeavor that demands dedication, creativity, and a relentless pursuit of excellence.

Chapter 8: Interviews and Insights

Conversations with Torvill and Dean

In candid interviews over the years, Jayne Torvill and Christopher Dean have provided a window into their world, offering insights into the highs and lows, the challenges and triumphs that have marked their journey in figure skating. These conversations not only illuminate the technical aspects of their performances but also reveal the emotional and personal dimensions that have defined their partnership.

Torvill and Dean often reflect on the genesis of their collaboration, tracing it back to their shared roots in Nottingham. The interviews shed light on the early days of their partnership, the challenges of breaking through in a sport dominated by traditional pairings, and the creative spark that ignited their approach to ice dancing. The evolution of their relationship from competitive partners to lifelong friends and collaborators unfolds in these conversations, providing a narrative arc that parallels their on-ice performances.

The duo's interviews also delve into the creative process behind their iconic routines. From the conception of the Bolero routine to the intricacies of their professional performances, Torvill and Dean share the inspirations, challenges, and moments of artistic breakthrough that shaped each routine. These insights offer a glimpse into the meticulous planning, experimentation, and collaboration with choreographers and musicians that went into creating performances that would captivate audiences worldwide.

Beyond the technical aspects, interviews with Torvill and Dean provide a glimpse into the emotional landscape of their careers. They speak candidly about the pressures of competition, the joy of Olympic triumphs, and the bittersweet moments of retiring from competitive skating. These conversations humanize the iconic duo, making their journey relatable to fans who have been touched by the magic of their performances.

Perspectives from Colleagues and Friends

Colleagues and friends of Torvill and Dean, whether from the world of figure skating or beyond, offer unique perspectives that enrich the narrative of their careers. Fellow skaters, coaches, and choreographers share insights into the collaborative process that defined Torvill and Dean's approach to their performances. These perspectives illuminate the dynamic interplay between technical precision and artistic expression that made their routines iconic.

Choreographers who collaborated with Torvill and Dean contribute valuable insights into the creative alchemy that unfolded in the process of crafting their routines. They speak to the duo's openness to experimentation, their ability to push the boundaries of traditional figure skating choreography, and the synergy that resulted from the fusion of movement and music. These perspectives provide a behind-the-scenes look at the artistic collaboration that produced performances that transcended the sport.

Fellow skaters, who witnessed Torvill and Dean's performances from the competitive arena, offer a unique understanding of the impact the duo had on the sport. Their reflections often touch on the transformative influence Torvill and Dean exerted, inspiring a generation of skaters to approach figure skating not just as a sport but as a form of artistic expression. These perspectives underscore the duo's role as pioneers who broadened the horizons of what figure skating could be.

Outside the realm of figure skating, friends and acquaintances provide glimpses into Torvill and Dean's personalities beyond the ice. These perspectives shed light on the camaraderie, humor, and genuine friendship that have been hallmarks of their partnership. The insights from colleagues and friends contribute to the multidimensional portrait of Torvill and Dean, showcasing not just their achievements on the ice but also the enduring impact of their personalities.

Fans' Reflections on the Duo's Career

The reflections of fans, perhaps the most intimate and emotional perspective, encapsulate the enduring impact of Torvill and Dean's career. Fans, who have followed the duo from the early days of their competitive performances to the present, share personal anecdotes, memories, and the profound emotional connections forged through the shared experience of witnessing their performances.

For many fans, Torvill and Dean's performances are not just athletic feats but moments in time that have left an indelible mark on their lives. Fan reflections often touch on the transformative power of watching the Bolero routine or the emotional resonance of their professional performances. These narratives speak to the universality of Torvill and Dean's appeal, transcending cultural and geographic boundaries to resonate with fans worldwide.

The impact of Torvill and Dean on fans extends beyond the ice rink. Their interviews, interactions, and the accessibility they have maintained with their admirers contribute to a sense of connection that goes beyond the typical celebrity-fan dynamic. Fans often express gratitude for the inspiration, joy, and sense of wonder that Torvill and Dean's performances have brought into their lives.

Moreover, the reflections of fans highlight the ripple effect of Torvill and Dean's influence on future generations. Many fans who were inspired by their performances have gone on to pursue figure skating, dance, or other artistic endeavors. These narratives emphasize the enduring legacy of Torvill and Dean, not just in the annals of figure skating history but in the personal journeys of those who have been touched by their magic.

In conclusion, interviews with Torvill and Dean, perspectives from colleagues and friends, and the reflections of fans weave together a rich tapestry of insights that enrich the narrative of their careers. These varied perspectives contribute to a holistic understanding of the duo's impact, from the technical brilliance of their performances to the emotional resonance they have created in the hearts of those who have been part of their remarkable journey.

Conclusion

The story of Jayne Torvill and Christopher Dean is a symphony of artistry, athleticism, and enduring partnership that has left an indelible mark on the world of figure skating. As we traverse the frozen landscapes of their careers, it becomes evident that their legacy extends beyond the ice rink, reaching into the hearts of fans, the annals of figure skating history, and the broader cultural tapestry.

Summing Up the Legacy

To sum up the legacy of Torvill and Dean is to embark on a journey through time, revisiting the elegant glides of their early performances, the breathtaking lifts of their competitive years, and the emotive storytelling of their professional routines. Their legacy is etched not only in the gold medals and accolades but in the collective memories of those who have been touched by the magic of their performances.

The legacy of Torvill and Dean is the Bolero routine, an iconic dance that transcended the boundaries of figure skating and became a cultural touchstone. It is the perfect scores at the 1984 Winter Olympics, a testament to their technical precision and artistry. It is the evolution of ice dance choreography, shaped by their willingness to push the boundaries of tradition and infuse storytelling into every movement.

Beyond the routines and scores, the legacy is the enduring impact on future generations. It is the young skater who watches a Torvill and Dean performance and dreams of gliding across the ice with the same grace. It is the artist who finds inspiration in their ability to weave narratives through movement. It is the fan who carries the magic of their performances as a cherished memory.

Torvill and Dean's Place in Ice Skating History

In the annals of ice skating history, the names Torvill and Dean resonate as a harmonious duet that elevated the sport to new heights. Their place in history is not solely defined by the medals they won or the routines they performed but by the transformative influence they exerted on the very essence of figure skating.

Torvill and Dean's place in ice skating history is marked by innovation. From the revolutionary Bolero routine to the seamless fusion of classical and contemporary elements in their professional performances, they redefined what was possible on the ice. Their impact reverberates through the choreography of subsequent generations, inspiring skaters to embrace creativity and storytelling in their routines.

Their place is also secured by their versatility. The duo seamlessly transitioned from competitors to professionals, captivating audiences with their artistic prowess in the world of show skating. This adaptability is a testament to their enduring passion for the sport and their commitment to exploring new avenues of expression.

Moreover, Torvill and Dean's place in history is enriched by their roles as mentors and ambassadors for figure skating. Through their involvement in Dancing On Ice and the Torvill and Dean International Skating Academy, they have become custodians of the sport, passing on their knowledge and passion to the next generation. Their impact extends beyond their own performances, shaping the future of figure skating through the skaters they inspire and mentor.

In conclusion, the Torvill and Dean journey is a testament to the transformative power of passion, dedication, and the pursuit of artistic excellence. As we close the chapter on their competitive careers, their legacy continues to unfold, inspiring new generations to glide, twirl, and dance on the frozen canvas of the ice rink. The story of Torvill and Dean is more than a chronicle of medals and routines; it is a celebration of the enduring magic that happens

when two individuals come together to create
art on ice.

Printed in Great Britain
by Amazon